Harmonica for Kids

How to Play the Chromatic and Diatonic Harmonica

By: Learning Time Press

This book is dedicated to the children of the world. May your hearts be full of joy.
If you enjoy the book, please consider leaving a review wherever you bought it.

Table of Contents

Introduction

What Is the Harmonica?

The harmonica is an instrument that has been capturing peoples' imagination for generations. Easy to learn, but with a wide variety of advanced techniques, the harmonica is a perfect introduction to music. No matter what age you are, you are sure to find something fascinating about this classic instrument.

A harmonica is made up of a wooden mouthpiece called a comb, with holes that you blow or draw air into. These holes lead to a reed plate, which, depending on whether you blow air into it or draw air from it, creates a different pitch. As a result of this, you can get a wide range of notes into a small instrument.

The reed plate contains the small, brass reeds, which are usually screwed to the plate and sit on top of the comb. The reeds at the bottom of the plate are responsible for the blowing notes, while the reeds at the top are responsible for drawing the notes.

Two cover plates hold the entire instrument together and help project the sound outwards. These plates usually have numbers engraved above the holes. We will use these numbers in our harmonica tablature to learn songs.

Inside each of these holes is a small metal reed. Depending on the length of the reed, a note is created as it vibrates against the hole. These reeds are arranged in various scales to determine the key of each harmonica.

Some harmonicas have 10 holes, while some have 12. Some have a button on the side that changes the pitch, and others are limited to one key. A common characteristic they all have is the instrument's signature, free-reed sound.

In this book, we will cover many different techniques and skills that you will need to play some of your favorite songs. This instrument is fun and easy to play for all ages. There's no better time to start learning than now!

Why Learn the Harmonica?

There are a lot of reasons to learn the harmonica. Learning music in general has been known to have many health and educational benefits. Here are just a few of the reasons to learn the harmonica:

It's Fun

The number one reason for learning how to play the harmonica is that music is fun and enjoyable. There is nothing quite like blowing a tune and having everything come together in perfect harmony. The harmonica is a great entry into the wonderful world of music.

You Can Play Along With Almost Any Song

As a result of how the harmonica's scales are arranged, there is almost no limit to the songs you can play along with. This makes it a great addition to virtually any ensemble. There are also many solo tunes that can be played with the right kind of harmonica.

It's Portable

You will never have to worry about where and how to carry or keep your instrument. It will always be right in your pocket. There are, of course, cases and protective equipment for your harmonicas, though, should you want to use them.

It Can Help Strengthen Your Lungs

The harmonica has been used in therapeutic applications to help patients improve their lung strength. The amount of resistance that occurs when blowing through the reeds is enough to exercise the muscles of the lungs and diaphragm. This can be helpful with all kinds of pulmonary issues.

It Can Improve Coordination

The hand-eye-coordination that is required to play the harmonica is applicable to all kinds of things. It requires kids and adults to make connections in their brains that they wouldn't have made otherwise. This is one of the reasons music is so good for our minds.

It Works With Any Type of Music

Rock, Jazz, Blues, Reggae; there is no end to the genres that regularly use harmonica in their ensembles. By learning it, you are opening yourself up to all kinds of musical styles and traditions.

It's Affordable

Many musical instruments are bulky, expensive and require a big financial commitment. This is why many people are reluctant to invest in an instrument that they may want to learn. A decent, basic, 10-hole harmonica, though, can be purchased for around ten dollars.

History of The Harmonica

Earliest Versions

The earliest version of the harmonica came from China thousands of years ago. Originally called the "Sheng," it was made with bamboo reeds instead of brass like in modern instruments. It was incredibly popular in traditional Asian music.

The Sheng made its way to Europe at the end of the 18th century, where its popularity quickly grew. In 1820, an instrument maker named Christian Friedrich Buschmann created "The Aura," which was a version of The Sheng, but with metal reeds. It only produced notes by blowing, but its loud sound set it apart.

In 1825, another instrument came on the scene with metal reeds like in the case of Buschmann's design, but with the ability to produce notes by both blowing and drawing. These went into production in Vienna in 1829 and became widely available all over Europe.

The simple design of the instrument meant that it was accessible to all kinds of craftsmen. Clockmakers particularly became adept harmonica makers, and many started their own lines of the instruments. One of these clockmakers was Matthias Hohner, who would go on to create one of the most well-known harmonica brands in the world.

Through Hohner, harmonicas were imported to Japan from Germany in 1896. There, they became known as the "Western Transverse Flute" and "The Mouth Harp." It was not until The Nippon Gakki Co., which later became Yamaha, began exporting harmonicas that they started to be known as their modern name.

Even though Yamaha eventually exported the instruments to America on a mass scale, Hohner was still responsible for its popularity at the turn of the century.

The Harmonica and The Civil War

The harmonica's popularity exploded when Hohner sent a few of his instruments to relatives who had emigrated to the United States. The harmonica became a major source of business for him. The price tag was a major contributor to its popularity, with most harmonicas costing only a dime at the time.

When the Civil War began, it became even more popular as a camp instrument. Camp instruments included things like the banjo, squeezebox, and other small instruments that could be carried on a pack. This gave the harmonica the perfect opportunity to shine.

Hohner even claimed that Abraham Lincoln himself played a Hohner harmonica. In one of their advertisements from the time, they claimed that Lincoln would carry a Hohner harmonica in his pocket at all times. According to them, Lincoln would often pull the instrument out and play it, saying, "This is my band; Douglas had a brass band, but this will do for me."

Of course, it's unclear where Hohner got this information, but by this time, the harmonica was ingrained in American culture. There are stories of Civil War soldiers playing the instrument to ease pain while experiencing an operation. It was a perfect instrument to store in a pack and pull out to entertain fellow soldiers around the fire.

By the time the Civil War was over, the harmonica had cemented its place in American Folk music. Its low price and easy playing made it perfect for any person on this earth to create music. It was truly an equal opportunity instrument.

The 1930's and the Blues

The harmonica continued to grow in popularity throughout the turn of the century. It was used on all kinds of recordings in many different genres. It began to blossom in the 1930s with the birth of the Blues.

The Blues emerged from African Americans in the United States and gained notoriety in the recording industry in the '30s and '40s. Musicians like Howlin Wolf and Muddy Waters took the harmonica to a whole new level. It was no longer just a simple folk instrument for playing around a campfire.

What these Blues musicians did was learn how to take the harmonica reed and bend the note by changing the shape of their mouths. This technique allowed them to bend notes down a half step or more. New notes were now attainable, and the possibilities were endless. We will learn this technique later in this book.

These musicians were the originators of a style known as the Chicago Blues. The Chicago Blues came about from musicians moving into urban areas during the great migration. The south's loss was the cities' gain, and this new style of expressive blues was born.

The Chicago Blues was characterized by these musicians' newfound ability to play indoors in clubs with electricity. This meant that the harmonica could now make use of amplifiers and P.A. systems. This loud, distorted sound is now heard all over modern blues albums.

We will focus on all kinds of harmonica playing in this book, but the Chicago Blues will be the basis for many songs and techniques. It's the most popular style of harmonica playing in modern music and fun for all ages.

Modern Music

The harmonica has found its way into all kinds of recordings throughout music history. Everyone, from The Beach Boys to Bruce Springsteen, has used the instrument to augment their sound. As a result of this, there are a lot of classic songs you can learn how to play.

A lot of modern music uses the harmonica for melodies, textures, and chords. Along with other free-reed instruments like the accordion and the harmonium, it fits in with all kinds of musical genres.

Fun Facts

Even Elephants Can Play

The harmonica is so easy that even elephants can play it! Shanthi, an elephant at the Smithsonian's National Zoo, has been known to play a tune on a harmonica attached to her stall. With a trunk of that size, she can get a big sound out of such a little instrument.

Many Presidents Played

Although we have covered Abraham Lincoln's affection for the harmonica, there were other presidents who enjoyed playing as well. Calvin Coolidge was also known to play a bit on the campaign trail. Later on, in the 1980s, Ronald Reagan joined the ranks of presidential harmonica players.

There Are Other Instruments by The Same Name

In the original German, the word harmonica actually refers to an accordion. However, since the sound and design are so similar, the names became interchangeable in translation. It was also the name of an unrelated instrument designed by Benjamin Franklin.

Benjamin Franklin Came Up with the Name

Founding father, Ben Franklin, invented an instrument that played music by running water over glass bowls. He called this instrument the glass harmonica from the Latin word, which means tuneful. Even though his instrument didn't catch on, the name continued as the instrument we know today.

It's the Most Popular Instrument

Harmonicas outsell every instrument, including guitars, worldwide. More than 40 million harmonicas have been sold in the U.S. alone. By learning this instrument, you are joining the ranks of millions of players!

They Can be Very Small

The smallest harmonica in production is the Hohner Little Lady. It only has 4 holes and can be used to produce 8 different notes. It should be noted that these harmonicas are very small and could present a choking hazard to younger children and toddlers.

There Have Been Huge Harmonica Ensembles

The largest ensemble of harmonica players was in 2009 in Hong Kong. About 6,100 people played the Guinness World Record Melody with an orchestra. This set the world record for the largest harmonica ensemble.

There Are Speed Players

In 2007, Santa Barbara resident, Nicky Shane, set the Guinness World Record for the fastest harmonica player. He played "When the Saints Go Marching In" at the breakneck speed of 285 beats per minute. Who knows, if you practice enough, you can find yourself breaking Nicky's record and ending up in the Guinness Book of World Records yourself!

Types of Harmonicas

Diatonic

Diatonic harmonicas are probably the most common type that you will come across. They are also the type recommended for the exercises in this book. They are the cheapest and easiest to play. They are the most widely available type of harmonicas no matter what part of the world you live in.

Diatonic harmonicas come in different keys and are tuned according to the Richter tuning. This means that all the holes will play notes that make up the chords and melodies in that key. You are not at risk of hitting a sour note with a Richter tuned diatonic harmonica as long as you are in the right key.

When selecting a diatonic harmonica, you will have to make a choice of one of twelve different keys. **For this book, we will be using a diatonic harmonica in the key of C.** This key and tuning will not only be the easiest to find, it will also work with most songs. We'll cover more on keys later.

A diatonic harmonica is smaller than its chromatic cousins. It has 10 holes with corresponding numbers engraved above them. When holding the harmonica, these numbers go on the top. More on holding the instrument, as well as more hand techniques later.

The diatonic harmonica is responsible for most of the playing you hear on recordings. Its universal tuning and easy playing make it perfect for all kinds of songs. If you hear the blues on the radio, odds are there is a diatonic harmonica somewhere in the mix.

Chromatic

Chromatic harmonicas are the more complicated counterpart to diatonics. They feature a lever on the side that will move the pitch of each reed up one-half step. This means that the chromatic harmonica can play any note on the scale regardless of the key.

While chromatic harmonicas have great qualities like being able to play a wide range of notes, they also have downsides. Their reeds are thicker, making them more difficult to bend and get a good, deep bluesy sound. They are primarily good for playing melodies and lead parts over an ensemble.

They are, however, great for sweet melodies and high-pitched parts that other instruments just can't play. The fact that they can play any note in the scale is a major plus when playing with a band. As a result of that, you can bring just one harmonica with you to band practice instead of several different ones for different keys.

Chromatic harmonicas are also quite a bit more expensive than diatonic ones. Since they are much more complicated, they are more expensive to make. This makes them a less than great choice if you are just getting started with playing.

It is better to pick a diatonic harmonica in one key and working your way up from there. After you learn some of the techniques and become proficient with the diatonic, you can make a move to chromatic. As with all musical instruments, it's all about building your skills overtime.

Tremolo

Tremolo harmonicas originated in East Asia and remain popular in traditional music today. The sound of the tremolo harmonica is somewhat different from the ones we covered, and the same techniques are not used. It has a sound on its own that is unique enough as it is.

The sound of the tremolo harmonica can only be described as having the quality of changing volume. As you blow into it, the volume seems to oscillate between quiet and loud without changing the air pressure. This effect is known as tremolo in many different aspects of music.

This harmonica gets its unique sound by having two reeds over each hole. One of the reeds is tuned perfectly, while the other is just barely out of tune. This produces the oscillating effect that sounds like the volume getting louder and quieter.

This effect happens because of something called beats. Beats are a physical phenomenon that happens when something is at a constant pitch, but the waveforms act against one another. This creates the illusion of changing volume.

Tremolo harmonicas are thinner and longer than standard diatonic instruments, though they also have 10 holes. The smaller designs allow players to play multiple harmonicas at once. By stacking the instruments on top of one another and blowing, players can create unique chords and lush sounds.

We will not be using the tremolo harmonica in this book. However, once you have mastered the diatonic, you can move on to tremolo and employ some of the techniques you know.

Octave, Chord, and Bass Harmonicas

Octave

Octave harmonicas have two reeds over each hole, just like the tremolo harmonica. However, these reeds are not slightly out of tune with each other; they are separated by octaves. In other words, they are the same note, but one is higher than the other. This produces a huge sound that won't work for every application but can be incredibly striking.

Chord

The chord harmonica is truly a marvel of engineering consisting of many different reed plates mounted on top of one another. The chord harmonica is capable of playing almost anything. This instrument is unique in a way that you are able to play all variations of chords, including minors and sevenths. This is much more versatile than a diatonic, but infinitely more complicated and expensive to play.

Bass

The bass harmonica is a huge instrument with 29 holes and is about the size of a football. The reeds on the reed plate are massive and capable of producing notes in a much lower register than any of the other harmonicas. It is very difficult to play and quite costly too. However, it's capable of making some of the wildest sounds that a free-reed instrument can make.

Final Thoughts

All of these harmonicas are interesting and capable of making beautiful music. However, they can't beat the beautiful simplicity of a 10-hole diatonic. **For the instruction portion of this book, we will exclusively use a 10-hole diatonic in the key of C.** This will keep us all on the same page and in perfect harmony (and melody).

Instruction

Holding the Harmonica

For Right Handers

It can be argued that how you hold the harmonica is the most important technique you can learn. The notes are easy to play, and if you are playing in the same key, you can't hit a wrong note at all. This means a lot of the sound depends on how well you hold it.

The professional, honking sound we hear when we think about blues harmonica comes from having proper hand technique. It's not easy to get it right the first time and may take a little bit of practice. You will know by the sound you're producing whether or not you are holding it correctly.

Step 1: "C" shape

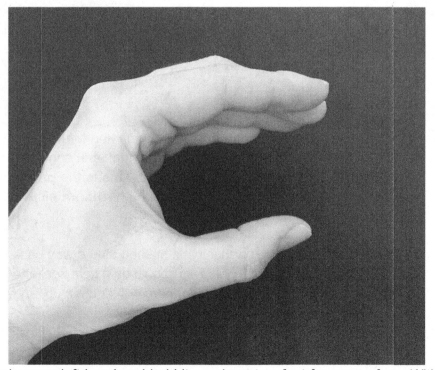

First, take your left hand and hold it up about two feet from your face. With your thumb and the rest of your fingers, cup your hand into a "C" shape. This "C" shape should be about the same width as your harmonica and should be held comfortably. Too tight, and your hand could easily cramp up.

It is especially important that you learn how to relax your hand in this position. It's usually first instinct to tighten up and try to hold it in position. This will make holding the harmonica in this position uncomfortable and difficult to maintain for a long time.

Step 2: Hold It in your left hand

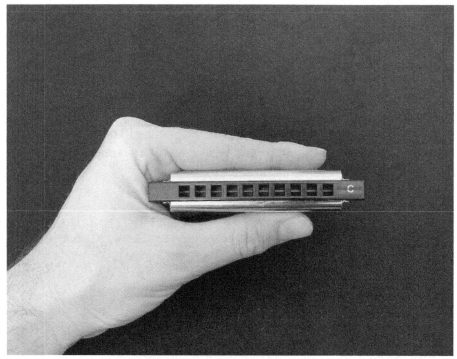

Take the harmonica and place it in between your thumb and forefinger in the "C" shape. You have to make sure that the numbers that are engraved on the instrument are running along the top from left to right. **This is the proper way to hold it and ensures that it will correspond with the harmonica tablature found in this book, as well as anywhere else.**

Make sure that the left side of the harmonica is pushed all the way back against the webbing of your thumb and forefinger. This should be a tight seal and may be uncomfortable at first. Eventually, the webbing there will toughen up, and you will be able to seal it with no issues.

Step 3: Align your hands

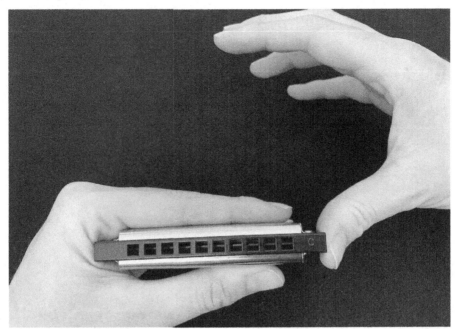

After you have placed the harmonica tightly in the "C" shape, place your right thumb on the right side of the harmonica. This will ensure that your hand is centered and in the correct place. It also gives you a little bit of leverage and more control when moving the harmonica across your lips.

The tips of your fingers on your right hand should be even with the knuckles on your left hand. With your thumb placed on the harmonica, you are now aligned to create a soundproof seal. This will help you make vibrato and other effects down the line.

Step 4: Cup Your Hands

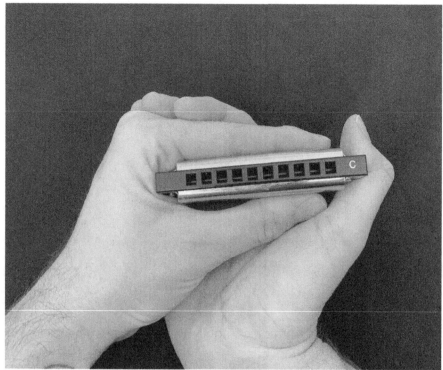

With your hands aligned, bring your cupped right hand down, hinging on your thumb placed on the side of the harmonica. Then, completely cover the backside of your left hand and the backside of the harmonica. Now any sound coming out of it will be muffled by your cupped hands.

Make sure that you practice getting the sound completely muffled with your hands. This may seem like an undesirable sound at first. However, practicing getting this right will help you with a lot of the techniques and playing styles that we will discuss.

Why a tight seal?

Getting a tight seal is important for getting a crisp, clean tone from your harmonica. Like many reed instruments, that is the most challenging part and the thing that requires the most skill. Just like with a saxophone or clarinet, the clearer your tone is, the better the sound will be.

This tight seal will help to muffle the sound in the same way that a trumpet mute does. We are all familiar with the "wah-wah" sound of a jazz trumpet. That is achieved by placing a mute over the bell of the horn. This does the exact same thing by cupping your hands and "muting" your harmonica.

Opening up your hands

After you have mastered getting the harmonica muted as much as possible, you can begin to practice opening your hands. Blow into the harmonica as you slowly open your hands, hinging your right thumb on the right side of the harmonica. You will notice an immediate change in the sound.

This change in the sound you notice is the effect of some of the higher frequencies being let out through the air. You can practice playing while opening and closing your hands at the same time. Hinge your thumb all the way out and get a wide range of motion. This same principle will apply when adding vibrato, but you must have complete control in order to do it effectively.

For Left-Handers

For left-handed harmonica players, it is going to be a bit more complicated. Many of the same things apply, but they are simply reversed. You will have to do a little bit more practicing in order to get a tight seal and a good vibrato sound.

Left-handers know that it is always going to be a little more difficult for them in a right-handed world. Unfortunately, it's no different with the harmonica. There is no such thing as a left-handed harmonica like there is with the guitar, so you will have to learn how to adapt.

For left-handed players, do all of the above steps, but with your hands reversed. For instance, hinge your left thumb on the left side of the harmonica instead of the right. It is important, however, that you make sure to keep the harmonica in the same position as the right-handers. Keep the engraved numbers running at the top from left to right at all times.

Due to how the notes on the harmonica are arranged, you may have a hard time getting a tight seal around the lower notes. This will make it harder to get the characteristic "wah-wah" sound of blues harmonica on those notes. By practicing getting that tight seal, you can set good habits right away and have an easier time with the more advanced techniques.

Hand Vibrato

We've all heard the vibrato effect, even if we didn't know what it was called. The vibrato effect is achieved when a tone pulsates, creating a wavy effect. This can be achieved in a wide variety of ways and is used on everything from the guitar to the human voice.

Vibrato is a key element of the Blues, especially Chicago Blues. It can sound mournful and can be used to imitate things and conjure up all kinds of feelings. With proper vibrato technique, you can easily make your harmonica wail like a mournful train whistle. This is very important for such an emotional instrument.

There are ways to achieve vibrato on the harmonica without using your hands. We will cover some of them later when we get to breathing techniques. The most popular and effective way to get the vibrato sound, though, is with your hands.

This is where getting that tight seal is the most important. Vibrato requires the sound to oscillate between muted, or "dark," and open, or "bright." This was demonstrated in opening and closing your hands by hinging your thumb on the side of the harmonica. With these hand vibrato techniques, we will use smaller movements in quicker succession.

Hand Vibrato Techniques

Squeeze Technique

This technique is the easiest for beginners. With your hands in the closed position, relax them so that the seal isn't completely closed. As you play, squeeze your hands together to alternate between a completely tight seal and a relaxed one. You will immediately hear the sound, then go between dark and bright.

The squeeze technique is good for beginners who are trying to understand the principles of vibrato. Although there will not be much of a range between the dark and bright sounds, it's a good start. Keeping your hands in the correct position at all times is a good first step. It will not only help you with your vibrato, but it will also help you with your hand position by keeping them together.

Pinkie Vibrato

This is the second easiest hand vibrato technique. It also allows you to keep your hands together and in the proper position. Furthermore, it allows for a reasonably wide range between the dark and bright sounds without much movement.

To do the pinkie vibrato technique, you will have to hold your hands in the closed position. Then, as you play, extend your right pinkie out and above your hand. Move it up and down as you play to get the vibrato effect. This method allows you to get a fast-moving vibrato that works well for all kinds of styles. Practicing it will also give you hand flexibility, which is incredibly important in harmonica playing.

Wrist Rocking

This is the most professional vibrato technique and the one you'll see frequently used by all the best Chicago blues musicians. It gives a deep oscillation between dark and bright and also gives a lot of control over your tone.

To do the wrist rocking technique, you'll have to use the hand that is not holding the harmonica. As you play, rock your wrist back and forth without moving the rest of your hand. This will create a small opening at the bottom of your cupped hands, which will allow more of the bright sound to come out.

It may seem like you shouldn't cover up the harmonica if you want it to be loud, but cupping your hands in a tight seal actually helps to project the sound. Instead of the air molecules dispersing everywhere, they are concentrated within your hands. This makes the sound louder and fuller.

This method gives you the most control and the crispest tone. It will also require the most coordination and takes quite a bit of practice to get it right. Once you do get this right, you will see a marked improvement in your tone. The sound is unmistakable and is a signature of the blues and harmonica playing in general.

Other Hand Techniques

There are a few other hand techniques that you can use to add color and expression to your harmonica playing. These are going to be a little more difficult to do correctly and won't be used in everyday playing. However, they are good to know and can come in handy for some special effects.

The Wave

For this effect, hold the harmonica in your cupped "C" shape hand. As you play, wave your hand in front of the instrument up and down, or side to side. This technique will literally disturb the air molecules coming out of the back of the harmonica. It will create a similar effect to a vibrato, but is much more wavy and extreme.

The Elbow Fan

With this technique, you will completely uncover and recover the harmonica to get the most extreme oscillation between bright and dark. With your hands cupped in a tight seal, pivot your arm at your elbow to completely release it. Pivot back and forth as fast or as slow as your elbow will allow you to. This gives a very extreme effect, but isn't very practical for blues or rock playing.

Final Thoughts on Hand Technique

When practicing your hand technique, you may be tempted to focus so much on getting it right that you let your hands cramp up. This is very common and shouldn't get you frustrated. You will quickly learn how to relax and hold the harmonica in a way that feels natural for you. Stretching your hands and fingers can be a great warm-up and will help you relax enough to feel comfortable.

It should also be noted that if you have a way to get a tight seal around your harmonica that is different from the one listed above, that is perfectly fine. As long as you can open and close the seal between your hands, you can achieve a good vibrato that will help you play the blues, just like all the legendary greats.

Breathing Techniques

While holding the harmonica is an essential aspect of playing, how you breathe might be more important. Think of your breath as a physical thing that is actually pushing the reeds. The same way you push the keys on a piano with your fingers, you do the same with your breath.

It may be difficult at first to think about your breath this way. You may even find out that you are running out of air quickly before finishing certain lines or chords. If this happens, don't worry. There are many exercises you can do to improve your breathing down the line.

There are a few things you can do right away to get your lungs in good working order. Getting plenty of exercise is the best way. Exercising regularly has been shown to increase lung health and capacity.

Another thing you can do is eat a lot of foods that are rich in antioxidants. Things like blueberries, strawberries, and raspberries can all help your lungs. Not to mention, these things are all delicious.

Your lungs are already incredibly flexible. They can be stretched and strengthened over time. However, you will be happy to know that you don't need a huge lung capacity to play the harmonica well. With a few techniques, you can use the breath that you already have to its fullest extent.

Air Management

One of the key techniques to learn when playing any wind instrument is air management. This means thinking about and regulating your breathing to be included with your playing. By combining the two, instead of thinking about them as different things, you can breathe more effectively.

The best way to manage your air with the harmonica is to think about breathing as drawing and blowing. Since the harmonica uses both inward and outward breaths, you can actually breathe through it as well. By doing this, you can keep your mouth on the instrument instead of taking it off to breathe.

Another way to get the most out of your air management is to breathe with your diaphragm. Many novice players breathe using their chest and shoulders. Imagine, instead, that you are grabbing a breath with your stomach from down on the ground.

By properly breathing with your stomach, instead of your chest, you are utilizing the full capacity of your lungs. Many people only use the top portion of their lungs by breathing with their shoulders. This can lead to you running out of air when playing long harmonica lines.

Music often requires you to think ahead. The harmonica is no different. You must plan on when you are going to take a breath with a draw note and exhale with a blow note. Since drawing and blowing produce different pitches, this is how you work your breathing into the music.

Circular Breathing

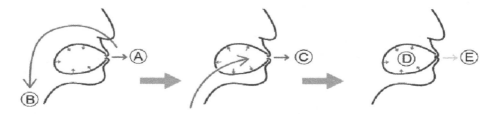

Circular breathing is an advanced breathing technique that was developed by the Aboriginal players of the Didgeridoo. This technique involves separating the muscles of your mouth and lungs. It is definitely not easy to do, but it can be learned, and for harmonica players, it is incredibly useful.

To do circular breathing, fill your mouth with air and exhale it slowly while inhaling with your lungs. To feel what this is like, puff out your cheeks and purse your lips to let the air out slowly. While you are doing this, inhale with your lungs through your nose. This will allow you to consistently blow a note almost indefinitely.

One good way to practice circular breathing is the straw exercise. To do this, put a straw in a glass of water and practice blowing bubbles in the water, at the same time, inhale through your nose. This is a good way to get a feel for the technique.

When learning circular breathing, the key is to separate your mouth and lungs. Many people have a bad habit of breathing through their mouths and connecting them. Circular breathing can help get them working independently again.

Since lung capacity and health are so important to the harmonica, circular breathing is a good option. It takes a long time to learn, but it can be one of the most useful things in your harmonica toolbelt. Long notes and sustain are the defining features of the instrument.

Breathing Exercises

There are several exercises you can do that will help increase your lung capacity as well. These exercises are incredibly easy, and the best part is, you can do them anywhere. Even small advances in your breathing technique can offer big rewards.

One such exercise is simply holding your breath. Just take a deep breath and hold it while standing. Hold it for as long as you can and do some stretches and twists as you do. Try not to hold the breath by closing your throat. Instead, relax and use your diaphragm. Be sure not to try to go too long, though. Just enough to stretch the lungs and stomach.

For another exercise, lie down on your back and place a large book on your stomach. When inhaling, try to get the book as high up as you possibly can. This will start to give you the muscle memory for breathing from your diaphragm.

Book Breathing Exercise

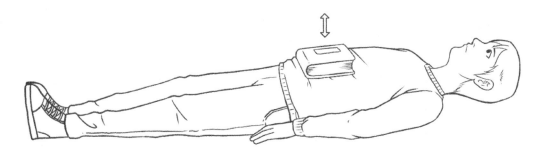

One of the best exercises for dynamic breathing that is required for harmonica playing is the candle exercise. To do this, light a candle (or have an adult do it) and blow on it for as long as you can without blowing it out. This will help you gain the breath control you need for more complicated harmonica parts.

Lastly, practice keeping your posture correct. Bad posture can lead to diminished lung capacity and can make blowing longer notes harder. If you are sitting, sit with your spine straight and your shoulders back. This will also help you not breathe with your shoulders.

Drawing and Blowing Technique

For the purposes of this section, we will be using the terms "blow" and "draw" quite a bit. These terms refer to the way the air is directed through the harmonic. When you blow on it, you are exhaling air through it, and when you draw on it, you are inhaling air through it. Knowing these terms ahead of time will be very helpful in these next sections.

Single notes

One of the most common ways to play the harmonica is as a single note, melody instrument. It's particular reedy, metallic sound is perfect for this. It is able to cut through the mix of any ensemble to play a melody that must get through.

When you first pick up the instrument, your first instinct will be to play a collection of notes. As you put your mouth on it, you will see that it covers a few of the holes. As you blow, you will produce the notes from all of these holes.

One of the first techniques you should learn is how to play just one note on the harmonica. There are a few ways to do this, and they will all have their time and place. By learning them, you will have a good foundation to expand on.

The most popular way to produce a single note is by adjusting the embouchure of your mouth. The embouchure is the shape of your lips as you blow out air. Depending on how wide or narrow you have your lips, you will provide air to a certain number of holes.

Practice adjusting your embouchure on and off the harmonica. Go from a wide oval shape and bring the centers of your lips together. When you do this with the harmonica, the instrument itself will be in the way. This will allow the centers to come together and cover any holes that you do not want to play.

Getting the embouchure right will not happen in one day. Many players are constantly perfecting their embouchure on all kinds of instruments. If you don't get it right away, don't give up. Eventually, you will be able to produce the single-note sound.

Tongue Technique

Another way that you can get just a single note from your harmonica is by using your tongue. Your tongue can cover holes that you do not want to play and leave the desired ones open. This technique also takes a lot of practice, but can yield some interesting results.

To practice the tongue technique, put the harmonica in your mouth, and play three notes together. Then, you can practice placing your tongue over each of the holes, one by one. You will hear as each note is eliminated and will get a feel for finding the holes with your tongue.

The tongue technique is useful and unique in that you can also block holes in the middle of your mouth. Normally, you can only play holes simultaneously if they are right next to each other. This is how you can achieve unique chords and note combinations.

Both of these techniques are great for learning how to play single notes. However, it is a much better idea to work on your embouchure than it is to rely on the tongue technique. Being able to play single notes by changing the shape of your mouth is much faster.

Chords

Chords are a collection of notes that create a unique sound altogether as one. Most rhythm parts of songs utilize chords to get a full sound that covers a lot of sonic ground. On the harmonica, playing chords is a great skill to have that will help you support the rhythm section.

Due to the nature of how the harmonica is tuned, there are natural chords located all over it. If you pick it up and blow into it, no matter what, you are producing an in-tune chord. This is one of the beauties of the harmonica; it is almost always in tune.

When blowing into the harmonica, no matter where you are positioned, you are blowing a C chord. Those notes on the blow side of the 10-hole harmonica are all tuned to C, E, and G. These three notes produce a C chord.

When drawing into the harmonica, you have more chord options:
- **G Chord** - Drawing into holes 1, 2, 3, and 4 produces a G chord
- **B Chord** - Drawing into holes 3, 4, and 5 as well as 7, 8, and 9 produces a B chord in a higher octave

- **D Chord** - Drawing into holes 4, 5, and 6 as well as 8, 9, and 10 produces a D chord in a higher octave.

All of these chords change if you change the key of your harmonica. However, the positions do not. Those hole combinations will always produce chords that work in the key the harmonica is tuned to.

Tongue Technique

Once you have mastered the tongue technique for single notes, you can work on using it to extend your chord options. There are different varieties of chord extensions that give a little extra dose of flavor to your music. These can be used to add unique sounds to the plain major chords.

For example, drawing into holes 1, 2, 3, and 5 will give you a B diminished chord which is useful in genres like Jazz and Funk. In order to achieve this chord, you must block hole 4 with your tongue. To get this sort of blocking, you will have to be able to be precise.

In order to get this kind of precision, scrunch up your tongue so that the tip is very small. With the harmonica in your mouth, try to get a feel for where the holes are and work on blocking just one. Once you are able to do this, try to do it as quickly as possible. This will allow you to add these notes as small flourishes and tasteful additions to your harmonica lines.

Bending

Bending is one of the most important harmonica techniques that a person can learn. Not only does it give you the ability to play new notes, but it is also the signature sound of the whole thing. The wailing, soulful sound that you typically think of with Blues harmonica are notes that are being bent.

Bending works by physically manipulating the reed with the flow of air. By pinching your lips and concentrating the air, you are changing the pressure. This change in air pressure will move the reed differently and gradually produce a different note. How big this variation in pitch is, depends on how much pressure is introduced.

The bending sound is absolutely essential to all kinds of genres of music. It provides the "human" element of the harmonica that has made it a staple of Folk music. Bends allow the instrument to be more like the human voice, with small variations in pitch.

Bending is also seen on instruments like the guitar. Again, it is primarily used in all kinds of music, but especially Blues and Rock. It is able to mimic the feeling and variations of the human voice. As a result of this, bending is usually associated with the soulful practice of making an instrument "talk."

Being able to bend takes practice. If you have taken the time to do the breathing exercises outlined above, it will be easier. Bending takes an enormous amount of lung strength due to the added pressure. Without having the right amount of breathing power, you will not be able to produce enough air to bend the note.

Draw Bend

The sound you most likely associate with bending the Blues harmonica would be the draw bend. This is because, on a diatonic harmonica, most notes can be bent on the draw. On these, holes 1-6 can be bent on the draw, while 7-10 are bent on the blow.

To do the draw bend, you must first lower your jaw slightly. Not enough to completely disengage from the instrument, but enough to loosen the grip. Then, raise the back of your tongue slightly. This will create a down current of air that adds more pressure to the airflow.

As you raise the back of your tongue, you'll want to narrow your embouchure as well. Not enough to completely block any holes, but enough to get a concentrated flow. This concentrated flow of air is what adds the pressure needed to bend the note.

When draw bending, you will actually be dropping the note's pitch. Usually, this is only about half a step, for example, from a G to a G flat. However, on the 3rd hole, it is possible to bend the note almost two-hole steps. Due to this, it is the note that you will most often hear bent on blues harmonica.

Once you start to get a feel for bending, you will be able to do it much easier. It's one of those things that is very difficult to do at first but gets much easier with time.

Blow Bend

On the diatonic C harmonica, you can blow bend on holes 7-10. This is a very similar principle to draw bending but can require a little bit more air concentration.

To blow bend, simply adjust your embouchure to only play one of the notes on holes 7-10. Then, lower your jaw just like with the draw bend. After that, you will raise the front of your tongue slightly instead of the back. This will put the focus of the airflow just behind your teeth.

Blow bends are definitely much harder to achieve than draw bends. They are also not nearly as common in Rock or Blues harmonica. They are most often used in pretty melodies or on a Chromatic harmonica. In fact, Stevie Wonder was a pioneer of blow bends on the chromatic, making it one of the most versatile harmonicas available.

Bending on a diatonic C harmonica is one of the most classic sounds you can get. So often, when we think about the Blues harmonica, we think about someone bending a note right at that third hole.

It's recommended that you try your hand at bending with that third hole draw first. It is the easiest reed to bend and will get you started on what it feels like to actually make the bend happen. Once you do that, you can move on to the others and eventually learn to blow-bend the highest notes.

Growling

Growling is another useful technique that is used primarily in Blues and Rock. With this technique, you can actually make the harmonica "growl" or shake with a vicious sound. This effect is heard on a great deal of older Blues albums from the classic era.

To achieve the growling effect, play a chord on your harmonica. Then, without closing your mouth, snort through your nose like you're making a pig-like sound. This will shake the reeds and give you that growl sound.

Think of this effect as a bit of snoring through the harmonica. You are using your sinuses to manipulate the flow of air through the harmonica. This will be a lot easier if you have learned to separate your mouth and lungs with circular breathing.

Practice making the snore-like sound with and without your harmonica. It is always easiest to switch between the two and practice the mouth formations like that. That way, you can get a feel for what it is like to make the shapes before adding the element of music to the mix.

This sound can be especially effective if it is combined with a bend. Like all techniques, it will also take some practice to be able to do them both at once. Once you can, though, you will be able to play along with some of the greats. With those two effects, you will be able to get the low-down, dirty harmonica sound that is so desirable.

Understanding Keys

In order for you to effectively play the harmonica, you must first understand the concept of musical keys. Keys are specific arrangements of notes on a scale that a piece of music is centered around. The harmonica, specifically, is dependent on keys to fit in with the rest of an ensemble.

Harmonicas are tuned to specific keys to make sure that they are always in tune. Diatonic harmonicas are always centered around the diatonic scale. This means that as long as your harmonica matches the key of the song, you will be in tune.

By understanding keys, you can also make decisions on which key you are going to use. Harmonicas can either be played straight or cross depending on the key. This means that for every key, you have a choice between two different harmonicas.

In this section, we will learn everything on how to find the key and the harmonica that fits it. We will also cover the difference between straight harmonica, cross harmonica, and some of the most common keys. By understanding how keys relate to music and the notes that your harmonica can produce, you can create interesting melodies and chords.

What is a musical key?

The musical key is the basis around which a piece of music is centered. Depending on the key, a piece of music will revolve around a group of certain notes. For example, a song played in the key of C major will use the notes C, D, E, F, G, A, and B. There are, of course, variations, but sticking to these notes means you will always be playing in the key of C.

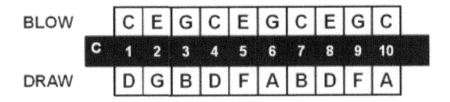

Why is this information useful? It's because if a group of musicians are playing together, someone can simply call out the key, and everyone will play in tune. This gives everyone a touchstone to revolve around. This technique is especially popular in Jazz.

This applies to the harmonica in that it is specifically tuned to certain keys. A 10-hole diatonic harmonica in the key of C major can play the notes C, D, E, F, G, A, and B. How you arrange those notes will determine how a piece of music sounds.

Keys can either be along the major scale or the minor scale. Whether a song is in a major or minor key will usually be determined by a few notes. For example, the C minor scale consists of C, D, Eb, F, G, Ab, and Bb. Most diatonic harmonicas only play in major keys, unless you are bending notes or playing cross harmonica, which we will discuss later.

Many traditional American songs and folk songs utilize major keys. For the purposes of this book, we will only be dealing with the major keys. As your skills progress, you can learn how to bend notes to turn the diatonic harmonica into an instrument that can play in a minor key. For now, we will focus on the keys that the instruments were meant to play in.

The best thing about trying to figure out if you're in the right key is that you will know right away. You will almost immediately be able to tell if your harmonica is in the right key for the song you're trying to play. It is very easy to hear when notes are fitting together. By understanding how this works, you can train your ear to hear it.

Finding the key

To fully take advantage of the harmonica's key system, you must learn how to find the right key. While this can usually be done just by listening, you can also figure it out in a couple of different ways. In this section, we will cover the best ways to find the right key.

When determining a song's key, you should first find the song's root note. The root note, or tonic, is the note that acts as the center of the scale. This note is what the key is named after. If a song is in the key of C major, the root note will be C. This can be incredibly useful in determining the key since the root note will often be the note a piece of music ends on.

One of the interesting ways to look at the root note or tonic is as a gravitational pull. All notes in the piece of music are pulled towards the center root note. Music can get further from the root note or closer to it, depending on how tonal or atonal the music is.

When music stays relatively close to this root note and the scale of the key, it's said to be tonal. This means that all the notes are in harmony together and run along the scale. If a piece of music does not follow this scale and gets further away from the root note, this is known as atonal.

Most music that will utilize the harmonica will be very tonal in nature. The harmonica relies on close root note relationships and adherence to the scales. This is what gives the harmonica its easy playability. However, chromatic harmonicas and certain bent notes on the diatonic harmonica can also be considered atonal if played properly.

Atonal notes and scales have their place in music. For the purpose of this book, however, we will not be dealing with anything that is not set along the diatonic scale. Instead, this will be left open for your experimentation later on. You will have plenty of opportunities to explore the possibilities of atonal music as you proceed on your journey.

Straight harmonica vs. Cross harmonica

Like many other wind instruments, a harmonica can be played in different positions. The first position is called straight harmonica. The second position is called cross harmonica. Learning both of these positions will allow you to play a wider variety of songs in one key.

Straight harmonica is usually associated with a prettier, more melodic sound. Whereas, the cross harmonica is associated with a grittier, more Blues-oriented sound. By becoming adept at both, you will have a deeper understanding of how the harmonica works and how every reed sounds.

Straight Harmonica

Straight harmonica is just as it sounds. This first position usually means that you are starting your lines on a blow note and ending on a draw note. This position relies heavily on exhale notes and uses inhale notes as accents.

Straight harmonica is used for types of music that stay in the tonal region. By relying mostly on the exhale notes, you will always get melodic, sweet-sounding harmonica lines. By playing the harmonica that is tuned to the same key as the song, you will always be playing in the first position.

Cross Harmonica

Cross harmonica is a way of "hacking" the keys of the instrument. To play cross harmonica, you must have an instrument that is 4 steps above the key that the song is. For example, to play cross harmonica to a song in the key of G, you must have an instrument in the key of C.

To play in the second position, you will start your lines on a draw note and end them on a blow note. This will give you the grittier, more Soulful sound that has become synonymous with Rock and Blues.

It may take some practice to learn which holes of the 10-hole diatonic harmonica sound the best to start and end lines with when playing in the second position. However, it can definitely give you some of the more professional-grade sounds that you might be used to hearing.

Most Common Keys

There are a few keys that are more common in American folk music and popular music. These keys tend to be more common because they encompass more notes that are found in other keys. This makes them more versatile and more open-ended musically.

For example, the notes found on the scale of the key of C major are also found in the scales of other keys. This means that a 10-hole diatonic harmonica in the key of C could also play along with songs in other keys. As long as you know which holes to play and which ones to avoid, this can be applied to almost any key.

Some of the most popular keys in American folk and popular music are the keys of C, G, and D. These keys tend to have the most common notes within their scales. As a result of this, they can be used with a wide variety of instruments. The keys of C, G, and D have almost every note within their scales.

Some keys share many common notes, so harmonicas in those keys can often be slightly interchangeable. For example, the keys of B and F# share many common notes in their scales. Due to these commonalities, you can effectively play harmonica in the key of B along to a song in the key of F#.

These commonalities in notes on the scale are what make the cross harmonica position work. This is how you are able to use the same harmonica for at least two different keys. Knowing that 4 steps down or up is a key with common notes could come in handy.

A couple of other common keys in American folk and pop music are the keys of A and E. These keys also encompass many notes that the others have as well. An important thing to remember is that there are only 12 total notes in music. How they are arranged and which ones are left out or included in a scale is what determines how a key sound.

What Keys to Get

As is stated above, we will mostly be dealing with the key of C for the songs and lessons in this book. This is because the key of C is perhaps the most common key of all. The scale of the key of C includes every non-sharp and non-flat note available. This means that it will be suitable for almost anything.

When starting out, most beginner harmonicas are going to be in the key of C. This, of course, includes only 10-hole diatonic harmonicas. Chromatic harmonicas also have keys, but this only determines the order of the notes. Since they can play any note in any scale, they don't have to be confined to any one key.

Once you have learned some of the songs and techniques laid out here, you may want to expand your palate of keys. A good start after a harmonica in the key of C is getting one in the key of G and one in the key of D. Once you have all three of these, you can play along with nearly any song.

After you have expanded that much, you can look into getting a harmonica in every key. This will allow you to be certain that you will never be left unable to play along with a song. However, this is not necessary since you can play nearly anything if you know the right techniques.

Once you have expanded your collection to the entire spectrum of keys, you can move on to chromatic harmonicas. Chromatic harmonicas are much more expensive and much more complicated. They add another element of hand technique in that you have to push and pull the lever. This is why it is recommended that you master the 10-hole diatonic first before adding an extra step.

In the next section, we will learn a few songs and utilize a few of the techniques we have learned. We will also learn how to read harmonica tablature and how to interpret different pieces of music. You do not have to know how to read music to learn how to read harmonica tablature. It is a completely different skill set.

Before moving on to the next section, make sure that you feel comfortable with all of the above techniques. This will ensure that you don't feel lost in any of the songs or lessons. There will be opportunities to execute things like bending and growling, so it will be best to know how to do them.

Easiest Ways to Play

Now that you have the basics of the technique and the musical principles down, you can now learn how you like to play. The harmonica is an incredibly diverse instrument that can be used in many different ways. With this, you may want to try many different ways of playing at first.

The arrangements listed here are by no means final. There are all kinds of ways that you can use the harmonica to play music. What instruments you play along with are entirely up to you. When it comes to music, always trust your ear and play what sounds good to you.

Solo

The harmonica is one of the few instruments that can be played solo in several ways. Solo means alone, or by yourself. Generally, this means that you are not playing along with any other instruments or people backing you up. It's a very common way for people to perform using the harmonica.

Solo can refer to playing by yourself without anyone else, but it can also refer to another common harmonica use. A solo is different from playing solo. When you play a solo, you are playing a free form melody part over other instruments. We will cover this later.

The nice thing about the harmonica is that you are able to play full chords and arrangements with it. You can play a chord part, followed by a melody that can make up an entire song. Trading off with this kind of call and response arrangement is popular in Blues and Folk music.

Another way to play the harmonica completely solo is to play a single-note melody on it. Single note melodies are the simplest way to play a recognizable tune. Many of the songs that we will cover later on in this book are single-note melodies.

While you can have a lot of fun playing the harmonica solo, it's even better with others. Music is about the connection between people and the unspoken bond of creating togetherness. The harmonica is perfect for this and allows you to play with all kinds of different musicians.

Duo

There are very few instruments that lend themselves to a duo ensemble, as well as the harmonica. The reedy, metallic sound resonates with many different types of instruments and can create a full sound. As a result of this, it is great for small bands or folk ensembles.

Perhaps one of the most popular duo configurations is the acoustic guitar and the harmonica. The characteristics of both of these instruments complement each other very well. Since the acoustic guitar is very percussive, it creates a strong backbeat for the harmonica's sweet-sounding melodies.

The harmonica and piano are other classic combinations. The piano also has extremely percussive qualities, just like the guitar, and the harmonica lies perfectly on top of that. Many piano players such as Billy Joel and Elton John have used the harmonica for this very reason.

This is not to say that the harmonica is not percussive. With the right kind of growling and breath technique, you can get a slightly percussive sound to play along with. This is great if you are playing solo and want a little bit of a backbeat or if you want to help provide one in a duo or ensemble.

Duos are great ideas for siblings, cousins, or friends around the neighborhood. A duo of guitar or piano and harmonica is a great way to get an introduction into the world of playing music with other people. It will help pave the way for more complicated ensemble arrangements and musical pieces.

Ensemble

The harmonica's light, breezy sound has been used in band and orchestral settings for over a century. It has a way of cutting through other instruments when it needs to and hanging back to support the rhythm when the situation calls for it. This versatility makes it perfect for playing along with others in all kinds of settings.

The word ensemble means a group of people. This can refer to actors, musicians, or just about anyone else. As a harmonica player, you are going to want to figure out what kind of ensemble you will want to play in.

You are able to play chords and rhythm parts on the harmonica, but it is much better suited for performing melodies. As a result of this, the ensemble is the perfect setting to let your playing shine. In a group of, let's say, piano, bass, guitar, and drums, the harmonica has a way of filling in the gaps and becoming the icing on the musical cake.

One of the reasons the harmonica lends itself well to ensembles is the way it is tuned. Since it is tuned to a specific key, it is difficult to play a wrong note. This gives you the ultimate sense of freedom and creativity when playing along with others. When you know you cannot make a mistake, you are able to have a lot more confidence and take more musical chances.

By having all the techniques and effects that you've learned ready and available, you can then use them when playing with an ensemble. This is the perfect time to stretch your musical wings and let the harmonica take you away.

One-Person Band

One-person bands have been around for centuries. There are reports of one-person bands showing up in the 1400s that consisted of a pipe and tabor. These are also known as a flute and a snare drum.

The first thing that comes to mind when you hear the term one-person band is a person with a drum on their back and a banjo. While this is not exactly what is meant by a one-person band in this context, there is a part of that setup that is very important.

A traditional one-person band setup uses a harmonica neck holder to hold the harmonica in front of your mouth. This makes it readily available to be played hands-free and leaves your hands to play one or two more instruments. This is why the neck holder is such a crucial piece of equipment for any harmonica player.

The one-person band is not just a novelty. Many famous, serious musicians have used the harmonica neck holder to accompany themselves on guitar or piano. Neil Young, Bob Dylan, and John Lennon have all been seen strumming guitars with a harmonica strapped to their shoulders.

With the neck holder, you are not just limited to playing guitar or piano. Since you have both hands and feet free, you could play percussion, keyboards, or more. The possibilities are endless, and with your harmonica skills in tow, you can make some beautiful music all by yourself.

Reading Harmonica Tablature

What is Tablature?

Tablature is a type of musical notation that is freely accessible to everybody. It makes communicating music easy and is commonly used nowadays instead of standard musical notation. With this, it is much easier to read and is available to almost anyone.

The word tablature means to tabulate or put something into a table or a chart. This is a good explanation of what tablature does for musical instruments. It translates the music into a chart that tells you what to do with your instrument.

Tablature is perhaps most commonly used on fingered instruments, such as the guitar or piano. In guitar or piano tablature, the charts show you where you should put your fingers as it relates to the piece of music. It takes out the extra step of reading the music and knowing the position.

For example, you don't need to know that placing your finger on the 5th fret of a guitar makes an A note. The tablature will just tell you to place your finger on the 5th fret. The chart is specifically tailored to the instrument, and you do not have to do the translation in your head as you do with standard musical notation.

Of course, with the harmonica, tablature does not tell you where to put your fingers, but rather where to put your mouth. The numbers in harmonica tablature correspond to the numbers above the holes on your instrument. This makes it very easy to read and translate what you are supposed to be doing.

Since we will be using tablature in this book, you do not have to worry about being able to read music. This can be a major barrier to learning a musical instrument for some people. You can rest easy knowing that you will be able to read the notated songs in this book with no problem.

Tablature Vs. Standard Musical Notation

There are some major differences between tablature, sheet music, and many reasons to use either. Lots of people are of the opinion that tablature is not the correct way to codify music. These purists believe that it will always be better to be able to read standard musical notation.

Being able to read standard musical notation or sheet music is an incredibly useful skill to have. Many professional musicians rely on sheet music to do their jobs and can read it by sight. This means that you can put a piece of sheet music in front of them, and they will be able to play it perfectly without even having heard it first.

The problem with this is that you must be able to look at the sheet music and then translate what you see to the fingering and mouth positions of your instrument. In order to learn how to do this, you must be as familiar with your instrument as you possibly can be. This is why a tablature is a good option for beginners to learn how to play. You do not have to do that extra translation step.

While being able to read music is a good skill, it is not entirely necessary. Many professional musicians don't know how to read music and rely primarily on playing by hearing. With enough practice, you will be able to play by ear as well. It is, by far, the most freeing and creative way to play music.

Between reading music and playing by ear, though, there is tablature. Tablature is a great way to learn how to play by ear and to see how mouth positions correspond with certain sounds. Learning tablature is the strongest first step you can take.

How to Read Harmonica Tablature

Harmonica tablature is one of the easiest types of tablature to understand and immediately begin playing along with. You don't need to know any kinds of special symbols or notation. It is actually even better if you do not know how to read music. This will allow you to read the tablature without being distracted by what you know about standard musical notation.

To read harmonica tablature, look at the chart. On it, you will see a series of numbers with a series of arrows underneath them. It will look something like this:

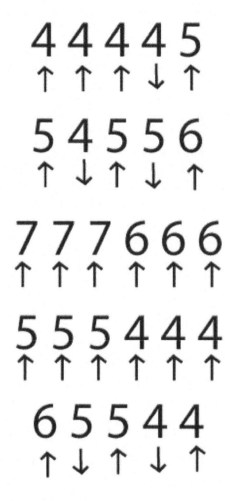

The numbers on the chart refer to the numbers that are engraved on the top of your harmonica. The arrows indicate whether or not you should draw on the hole or blow on it.

Harmonica tablature will tell you whether you should be using a diatonic or chromatic harmonica. They will be written specifically for that instrument and should say so at the top. It should be noted that tablature for a diatonic harmonica will not translate over to a chromatic one.

Tablature also does tell you what the rhythm of the notes should be. It is very helpful for you to know how a song sounds like before you start to learn it with tablature. This is one way that standard musical notation is slightly better despite being more difficult to learn.

How to Play Along to Tablature

While it is entirely possible to do what is called sight reading with tablature, it is still very difficult. Sight-reading means that you can look at the chart and play it right away without practicing first. This is difficult by any standard, but made even more difficult by tablature's lack of rhythm notation.

Most people will have to spend some time with a piece of harmonica tablature before they can play it with precision. If you cannot play a piece right away, don't be discouraged. It will take many months of practice before you are able to sight-read anything, and even if you never learn, that is okay too.

The best way to learn a piece of harmonica tablature is to practice it slowly at first. The trick is to engage something called "muscle memory." Muscle memory means your mouth will automatically go to the place it's supposed to just by virtue of practicing.

After you have gone through methodically and learned how it feels to play the piece, you can try speeding it up. Don't rush this part. The point is to get your brain to learn exactly where your muscles are supposed to go and have them move there as an automatic process.

Harmonica Songs for Kids

Ages 0-3

Row, Row, Row Your Boat

A staple of early music learning, Row, Row, Row Your Boat is a simple song to play. This song was written in 1881, but the words have probably been around for a whole lot longer. It is a nice song with a beautiful melody and lends itself well to do "in the round." It will blend in perfectly on any field or camping trip.

When playing, notice the descending "merrily, merrily" section. This should be relatively easy to play on your 10-hole diatonic harmonica. The melody line goes down the instrument in a straight line and follows the engraved numbers at the top of the instrument. This is what makes it one of the easiest songs to learn.

4 4 4 4 5
↑ ↑ ↑ ↓ ↑

5 4 5 5 6
↑ ↓ ↑ ↓ ↑

7 7 7 6 6 6
↑ ↑ ↑ ↑ ↑ ↑

5 5 5 4 4 4
↑ ↑ ↑ ↑ ↑ ↑

6 5 5 4 4
↑ ↓ ↑ ↓ ↑

Mary Had A Little Lamb

Another popular song for children just learning how to play music is Mary Had A Little Lamb. It is also very easy to play on the harmonica. This is another old song from the 19th century with lyrical roots going even further back. It has been a cherished nursery rhyme for many, many years.

This song is based on the true story of Mary Elizabeth Sawyer, who had a pet lamb that she brought everywhere. It even followed her to school! Sing along with the melody in your head as you play, and it will help you get a feel for where all the notes lie on the harmonica.

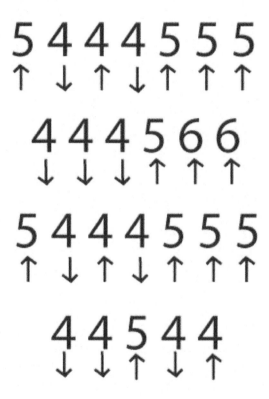

Twinkle Twinkle Little Star

Twinkle Twinkle Little Star is a tune that almost everybody knows right off the top of their head. Written by the poet Jane Taylor, the words to this song were published in 1806. However, the tune is also shared by other beloved children's songs such as Bah Bah Black Sheep and The Alphabet Song.

Many people believe that the tune was composed by Wolfgang Amadeus Mozart as a child. While Mozart did compose many songs that are now a part of our collective culture, this was not one of them. As it turns out, it is a complete mystery who actually came up with this classic melody.

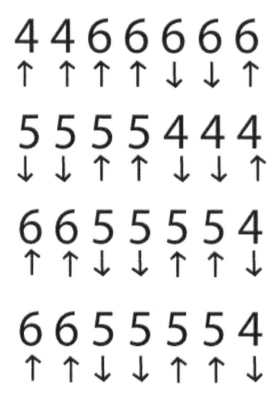

Oh Susanna

With roots in a darker American past, Oh Susanna has made its way into the American canon of music. With modified new lyrics, it has been used to teach the C major scale for years and years. It is a great way to learn how the different draw and blow functions work on the scale of the instrument.

While this little tune can easily be played solo, it sounds especially good as a part of a duo with a banjo or a guitar. If you can memorize the melody part and play it over a chord progression, there's no better sound in all of music. You can add holes as you play to expand the melody as well.

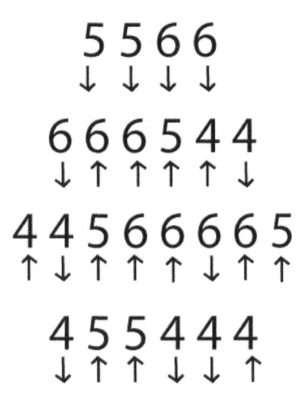

Jingle Bells

This is one of the most quintessential Christmas songs in the history of music. Jingle Bells is a must-learn for the holiday season. It is perfect for playing around the fire and leading the family in a sing-along. On top of that, it is very easy to play due to its repeating notes and little variation.

It might seem hard to believe, but Jingle Bells was not originally supposed to be a Christmas song. If you think about the lyrics, you will realize that never once does it mention Christmas or the holidays at all. It just goes to show that music has a way of surprising you no matter how long you've known a song!

5 5 5 5 5 5
↑ ↑ ↑ ↑ ↑ ↑

5 6 4 4 5
↑ ↑ ↑ ↓ ↑

5 5 5 5 5 5 5
↓ ↓ ↓ ↓ ↓ ↑ ↑

5 5 5 4 4 5 4 6
↑ ↑ ↑ ↓ ↓ ↑ ↓ ↑

Ages 4-7

Amazing Grace

Amazing Grace is widely accepted to be one of the most beautiful songs ever written. Widely used for many religious purposes, this song is not just relegated to church. It is a perfect tune to have in your back pocket for any occasion and is always welcome when the mood happens to strike you.

Written in 1773 by John Newton, this song has roots in the Christian religion, but has been used all over the world. As a result of this, it is instantly recognizable no matter where you go and what occasion you happen to find yourself in. It is a very useful song to know and has many fans all over.

6 7 8 7 8 7 6 6
↑ ↑ ↑ ↑ ↓ ↑ ↓ ↑

6 7 8 8 8 9
↑ ↑ ↑ ↑ ↓ ↑

8 9 9 7 6 6 7 6
↑ ↑ ↑ ↑ ↑ ↓ ↑ ↑

6 7 8 8 8 7
↑ ↑ ↑ ↑ ↓ ↑

On Top of Old Smokey

On Top of Old Smokey is a traditional American classic that has unknown origins. It is believed that it was written sometime in the 1840s and is a reference to the Great Smokey Mountains in Tennessee and North Carolina. Unless, of course, you are more familiar with the version entitled On Top of Spaghetti.

It has been played by folk acts like Pete Seeger and The Weavers. Due to this, it is instantly recognizable as an American classic. This will make it a welcome addition to any campfire sing-along or road trip jam session, especially when paired with a guitar or banjo.

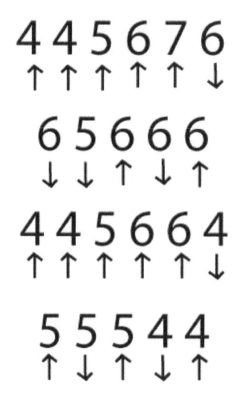

Alouette

Alouette is the first non-American song in our songbook. Like so many early songs, its origin is unknown, and the tune has been passed down through the generations. Most people believe that the origin of the melody is French Canadian. This is due to the lyrical content of the song in the fact that it has become an unofficial national song of French Canada.

50

The lyrics of the song describe the steps involved with hunting a lark, which is a type of game bird. Early colonists ate larks, and they were a staple for French Canadian fur trappers. This is the basis for the theory of the song's French-Canadian origin.

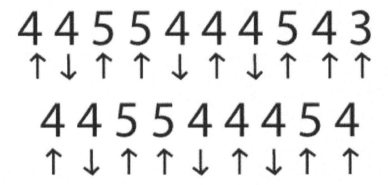

This Old Man

This Old Man is a popular song for teaching children counting. It has tongue-twisting lyrics and nonsensical words that make it fun to sing and fun to play with on the harmonica. The song was first published in 1906, but has been traced back to Wales in the 19th century, where it was established for many years before making it elsewhere.

This song has a very rhythmic cadence that can be very well suited for the harmonica. It is a great song that can be used to practice your staccato rhythms. To do this, use your tongue to start and stop the flow of air through the harmonica. This can be done on both a blow note and a draw note.

6 5 6 6 5 6
↑ ↑ ↑ ↑ ↑ ↑

6 6 5 5 4 5 5
↓ ↑ ↓ ↑ ↓ ↑ ↓

Ages 8-11

Home On the Range

Home On the Range is perhaps one of the most popular folk songs in all of American history. Written by Brewster M. Higley from Kansas, this song was the unofficial anthem of the American West. With this, it is perfect for camping trips and is instantly recognizable as an outdoorsy tune.

Home On the Range has been used in all kinds of movies and television shows and was even adopted as Kansas' official state song in 1948. It is inextricably linked to America and the development of the Wild West. It is a simple little tune, and an absolute must-learn for any cowpoke out on the open prairie.

4 4 5 5 6
↑ ↑ ↑ ↓ ↑

5 4 5 6 6 6
↑ ↓ ↑ ↓ ↓ ↓

6 6 7 4 4 4 3 4 4
↑ ↓ ↑ ↑ ↑ ↑↓ ↑ ↓

Joy To the World

This exuberant Christmas carol has the distinction of being the most published Christmas song in North America. This makes it a perfect tune to learn in order to get ready for the holiday season. It is joyful and beautiful, which suits the harmonica perfectly and is sure to enhance holiday sing-along.

While it may be tempting to open your mouth and play several notes at a time, it is important that you maintain your embouchure. This will give you crisp notes and a clean tone that is desirable for this kind of major key melody.

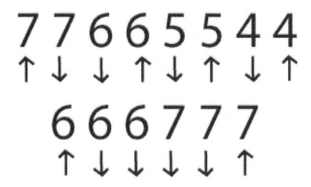

Lean on Me

Lean on Me was originally written and recorded by the singer-songwriter, Bill Withers, in 1972. It has been used in all kinds of movies and television shows and was a number one single in 1972 for three weeks. There have also been many other versions recorded that have been massive hits as well.

This song is especially interesting due to its use of the C major scale. You'll notice that it cascades up and down in a very linear way. Learning this song is a perfect way to master what the scale sounds like and make you more comfortable improvising around the instrument as you get better.

My Girl

The sweet melody of My Girl is a nostalgic trip down memory lane for anyone, even if you're hearing it for the first time. Learning this song is sure to impress any oldies fan or music lover of all types. With an original melody and lyrics by Smokey Robinson and Ronald White, it was written as an ode to Smokey's wife, Claudette.

This song is played on the very top register of the diatonic C harmonica. As a result, it could be best played as a duo with a guitar, piano, or banjo backing. This will allow the higher notes to cut through and still have the rhythmic backing of the other instruments to keep the pace and move the song forward.

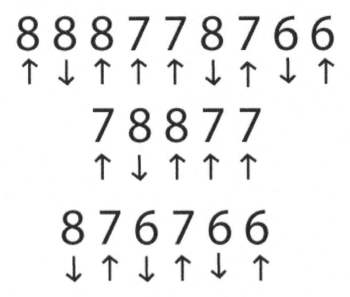

8 8 8 7 7 8 7 6 6
↑ ↓ ↑ ↑ ↑ ↓ ↑ ↓ ↑

7 8 8 7 7
↑ ↓ ↑ ↑ ↑

8 7 6 7 6 6
↓ ↑ ↓ ↑ ↓ ↑

Silent Night

This German folk song has become a beloved Christmas carol for people all around the world. Bing Crosby's version in 1935 is the fourth best-selling single of all time, and the song has been covered all across genres and recording artists. This makes it a great tune to learn and add to your collection of Christmas tunes.

This song is a little bit more difficult to play due to the range of notes. It has an unusual arrangement of draw notes and blow notes and may take some practice to get right. It is deceptively simple.

6 6 6 5 6 6 6 5
↑ ↓ ↑ ↑ ↑ ↓ ↑ ↑

8 8 7 7 7 6
↓ ↓ ↓ ↑ ↑ ↑

Ages 12 and Up

Somewhere Over the Rainbow

This beautiful song from The Wizard of Oz was written by Harold Arlen and was originally sung by actress Judy Garland. It is instantly recognizable and a quintessential part of the American songbook. It has also been the inspiration for many other songs throughout history. Without Somewhere Over the Rainbow, there is no Starman by David Bowie.

This is a fairly complex song with a wide-ranging melody all over the instrument. Be sure to always start in the first position and know where the numbers are at all times. This will help you keep track of where you are positioned in correspondence with the tablature.

4 7 7 6 6 7 7
↑ ↑ ↓ ↑ ↓ ↓ ↑

4 6 6 4 6 6
↑ ↓ ↑ ↑ ↓ ↑

5 5 6 6 4 3 4 4 5 4
↑ ↓ ↑ ↓ ↓ ↓ ↑ ↓ ↑ ↑

Hey Jude

This song, written by Paul McCartney and performed by The Beatles, is a classic rock staple that isn't often played on the harmonica. It is most notable as a piano song, so using the harmonica is a fresh take that any music fan can appreciate.

This is a great example of the harmonica being played in the cross position. While *Hey Jude* is technically in the key of F, the C major diatonic harmonica is perfectly suited for playing it. Learning this song is a great way to learn how all the keys intersect.

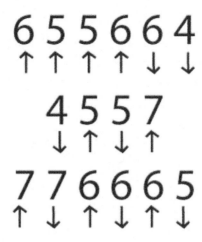

Yesterday

Another Beatles song written by Paul McCartney, this song is also in the key of F. It is another fantastic example of how the C harmonica can be used to play almost any song in virtually any key. It is an incredibly versatile instrument that can be used for all kinds of applications.

This is one of the more wide-ranging tunes we have in this book. It uses hole 4-7 for the main melody, which is a fairly large distance to travel on the harmonica. With this, you need to make sure that you are comfortable accurately moving the instrument around on your mouth as you are practicing it.

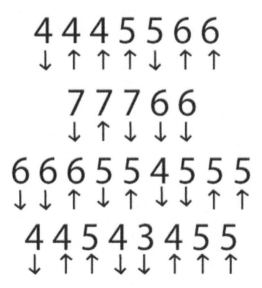

Taps

This traditional melody is generally used at military funerals and other solemn occasions. It is synonymous with honoring the fallen and is a beautiful melody to boot. Ideally, you won't ever have to use it, but it is a good idea to know this song so that you can appreciate its delicate simplicity.

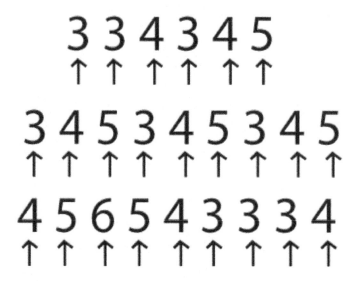

Frankie and Johnny

Frankie and Johnny is an American ballad, which is about two lovers who are caught on the wrong side of the law and each other. This is the most difficult melody to play out of all the songs in this book, requiring some practice to get the parts right. If you have mastered all of the above songs, though, this one will prove to be no problem at all.

4 4 5 6 6 5 4 4
↑ ↓ ↑ ↓ ↑ ↑ ↑ ↑

4 4 5 6 6 5 4
↑ ↓ ↑ ↓ ↑ ↑ ↑

4 5 6 6 7 8 6 7 7
↑ ↓ ↓ ↓ ↑ ↓ ↓ ↑ ↑

6 7 7 7 7 7 6 6
↓ ↓ ↑ ↑ ↑ ↑ ↓ ↓ ↑

5 5 5 4 5 4 5 5 4
↑ ↑ ↑ ↓ ↑ ↓ ↑ ↑ ↑

Conclusion

Other Instruments to Learn

Now that you know how to play the harmonica, you might start looking around at other instruments you would want to learn. There is such a wide array of musical instruments out in the world, and the principles of the harmonica apply to many of them. The more instruments you learn how to play, the easier it will be to learn even more.

One instrument that translates well to the principles of harmonica is the piano. The piano's white keys are set up very similarly to the holes on a diatonic harmonica in the key of C. As a result of this, it will be a familiar sound to you, and you will be able to pick notes out much easier than someone who does not know how to play the harmonica.

Another very similar instrument is the accordion. The accordion has a piano-style keyboard on the side that has the same diatonic C configuration. It also uses the same principle of blowing wind over reeds to make its signature sound.

If you learn how to play particular notes on a piano keyboard through the harmonica, you can play any keyboard instrument. This includes things like the melodica, harmonium, and even synthesizers. The harmonica is a great stepping stone to all these wonderful instruments.

Teaching Others

As a musician, it is now partly your responsibility to help teach others and give them the gift of music too. Teaching other people how to play the harmonica can be a fun and rewarding experience. It can also make you a better player and force you to explain certain principles.

This book is an excellent start to teaching someone how to play the harmonica. The techniques outlined here will translate to almost anyone. Since it is the one you learned from, it makes sense to use it to teach your friends.

You can also swap lessons. If you are interested in learning how to play the piano and you have a friend who knows how to play the piano, you can offer to trade lessons. This is a great way to share skills and gain some extra-musical knowledge.

When teaching others, remember to be patient. Everyone learns at their own pace and needs their own time to be able to understand concepts and techniques fully. Surely, you weren't able to play all the songs and do all the techniques in this book right away. It is important to remember that others won't be able to either.

Friendship Through Music

Music has a wonderful way of connecting people. By sharing the gift of music, you are expressing yourself together along with a group of other, like-minded people. That is a great way for friendships to blossom.

There are usually opportunities at school or in your community to get together with other people and play music. The harmonica is a unique instrument that isn't going to be as popular as some other instruments. As a result of this, harmonica players are always in demand.

Another great way to make some friends through music is to start a harmonica club. Since the instrument is so cheap and freely available, it is a great way to start a club and get people together. You can have weekly lessons and jams that are sure to build camaraderie and friendship along the way.

Some of the best friendships are made through music. If you are not someone who is necessarily athletically inclined, music is a great fallback. You are sure to find some strong friendships and form bonds that will last a lifetime.

Final Thoughts

In this book, we have covered every aspect of playing the harmonica for kids. Hopefully, you have learned enough that you feel confident and excited about getting out and playing. That is the real point of learning how to play music.

There are many lessons in this book, but the one that you should take away the most is to be patient with yourself. Learning something doesn't happen overnight. It doesn't happen in a week. It might not happen in a month.

The point of the entire process is the process of learning itself. Learning how to play music should be full of discovery. It should not be something that you dread doing. If you find yourself not wanting to practice as much, take a break. You can always come back to it.

As you are learning, you should also be listening to as much harmonica music as you can. There are so many resources on the internet for finding music. Find something that excites you and makes you want to play and then learn how to play it.

Music is one of the most rewarding things that a person can learn. It has a way of making its way from your ears down into your heart. Being able to be the person who makes that music is truly a gift and one that will serve you well throughout your life.

Made in the USA
Coppell, TX
02 September 2021

61715249R00039